DIARY

OF A

MINECRAFT CREEPER

Book 3

Attack of the Barking Spider

by Pixel Kid and
Zack Zombie

Friday

Today was the last day of school. . .and I'm so excited!

HSSSSS.

There isn't much I'll miss about school, though.

Teachers. . .nah.

Homework. . .nah.

The only thing I'm gonna miss is lunchtime.

Not because of the food...Blech!

It's because I won't be able to hang out with my best friends, Harry, Ed, Fred, Ned and Jed until after the holidays.

1

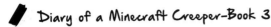

It's always fun to hang out with those guys. We've all been friends pretty much since kindergarten.

"Are you guys going anywhere special over the summer vacation?" asked Ed.

"Nah," said Jed.

"Nope," said Fred.

"No," said Ned.

. . .All at the same time.

Man, having a Wither as one of your best friends is really cool. The only problem is getting used to the echo. . .echo. . .echo. . .

Anyway, Fred, Ned and Jed recently started asking us to call them 'One Explosion.'

Don't ask me why.

But, I think it had to do with some bad chili they ate last week.

Nasty.

"My mom and dad said they planned a surprise trip us," shrugged Harry. "What about you, Ed?"

"Nothing. But I guess I can make plans with. . .uh. . .One Explosion."

Yeah!. . .Yeah!. . .Yeah!

"How about you, Jasper? You going anywhere for summer vacation?" Ed asked me.

"Yeah! I'm going to. . ."

RIIINNNGGG.

The lunch bell went off, so we gathered our stuff and went to class.

Man! I never got to tell my friends about my really cool summer vacation plans.

You know, our group of friends has gotten bigger since drama night. That's because now Burt the Creeper and his gang hang with us sometimes.

Blake the Zombie and Fred, Ned and Jed. . .
I mean One Explosion. . . get along really
well. . .

They mostly just grunt at each other. . .in
stereo.

Well, anyway, my holiday plans are going to
be awesome!

My family and I are going on a camping trip
to the Forest Biome Caravan Park.

Yeah!

Once a year, my parents take us to this
caravan park for a week. They said something
about trying to get us away from all the
'technology.'

I have no idea what they're talking about.

But I do like getting away. It's fun to spend time with my family and get away from it all. . .but I'm definitely going to miss my friends.

Anyway, I've made a list to help me pack:

- Shovel (In case I want to build a sandcastle. . .or go poop) – Check!

- Swimming girdle (basically swim trunks for Creepers) – Check!

- Pumpkin pie (Mom made some extra. So I snuck some in my backpack. . .Yum!) – Check!

And last but not least, my diary. . .err, I mean journal.

I am so ready for summer vacation!

GRRRRRRRRR.

Ugh! You know, my stomach has been feeling really weird lately.

GRRRRRRRRR.

Prrrfft.

It all started a few weeks ago when a new transfer student started at our school.

Her name is Tibia McRib, and she's a Skeleton.

And she's one of the most beautiful mobs I have ever seen.

HSSSSSS.

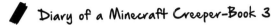

So, anyway, ever since she's been around, my stomach has been feeling really weird.

Like, one time, Tibia came by to say hi and my stomach rumbled so loud that they had to evacuate the school.

Yeah, somebody called the police about a wild animal on the loose.

They even called the bomb squad too.

Figures.

Saturday

We packed all our camping gear into the car and left the house before the sun even rose. Dad is huge about beating the holiday traffic.

In the car, my little brother Seymour went straight back to sleep. Ima and I were awake in the back seat of the car with our parents in the front.

GGGRRRRRRAAAAAWWWWRRRRR.

"Seriously, Jasper?" Ima said, rolling down the window.

"Uh. . .sorry."

"Oh, Jasper, was that your stomach?" gasped Mom.

"Woah, kiddo! Do you need a toilet break?" asked Dad.

9

Urgh.

"Uh...I'm all right. I've had a bad stomachache for the past week or so..." I said.

"A week? That's CRAZY," shouted Ima.

"Sounds like you've got the bubble guts," my Mom said.

"Honey, it reminds me of the bad case of bubble guts I had when I first met you," my dad said.

Oh boy...Here we go with another story.

"It was just like yesterday when I was young Creeper and I saw the most beautiful Creeper sneaking up on a player silly enough to go mining at night."

"Tee, hee," Mom let out a giggle.

Ima and I groaned.

We've heard this story SOOOO many times. It's the story about how my parents first met.

Blech!

But Dad continued, "...I went home, and I had the worst bubble guts ever! All I know is that the pipes in our house were never the same after that," Dad said with a weird grin.

"EWWWWW!"

"Oh, my gosh! I know what it is!" yelled Ima. "Jasper's got a crush!"

"HA, HA, HA, HA, HA!" I laughed, trying to make believe like I understood what Ima was talking about.

"Jasper's got a crush! Jasper's got a crush!" sang Ima.

"That would explain all that time you spent in the bathroom these past few days," my Mom said.

Wait. . .what?

"Jasper, if you keep messing with your hair in the bathroom, it's going to fall out," my dad said.

That's my dad's favorite line.

It's like if I do anything for too long, it'll fall out.

"If you keep picking your nose, it'll fall out. . ."

"Or, if you keep biting your nails, they'll fall out. . ."

"Or, if you keep playing with your belly button, it's going to fall out. . ."

"Or, if you keep playing with those skeletons, a record is going to fall out. . ."

So, wait a minute. . .does that mean if I fart too much, my butt's going to fall out?

My family is so weird sometimes.

We were about halfway to the campgrounds when it was almost lunchtime. Dad drove to a nearby park, and we set up a picnic.

I hopped away to nice quiet spot where I could enjoy my pumpkin pie when suddenly. . .

"Pssst," came a voice from behind a tree.

Whoa, I've never seen a talking bush before.

So I turned around and hopped over to the talking bush.

"Hello, Mr. Bush, would you like some pie?"

"Dude, it's me, bro!" whispered the bush.

Uh, I can't say I recognized the bush, but it acted like it knew me.

"Hey. . .what's up bush-dude?"

Then Steve jumped from behind the bush.

"Oh, hey, Steve. I thought I was having a religious experience there for a second. So, what are you doing here?"

"Dude, I heard you were going on vacation and I wanted to tag along," Steve said.

"Oh, man, I'm so glad you're here. Something really weird is happening to me, and I need your help to try to find out what it is."

So I explained my symptoms.

Steve raised one eyebrow. That normally means he's confused.

Man, eyebrows are so weird.

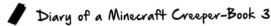
14

I remember one day, I really wanted to see what it'd be like to have eyebrows.

So Steve found two caterpillars in the forest and stuck them on my face.

Creepers don't look good with eyebrows. Especially squirmy, hairy ones.

Don't even get me started on Villagers. . .

Anyway, then I started telling Steve about what Ima said.

HSSSSSSSSSSS.

"Whoa, calm down, dude!" Steve said as he slowly walked behind a tree.

"Breathe, dude, breathe. . . So, what's the matter?" Steve asked me.

"Hey, Steve, what's a crush?" I sighed.

Steve's eyes got really wide.

"Oh. I thought you were going to talk about something really serious. Like a death in the family or something," said Steve.

"Oh, nah. We have plenty of those."

"Seriously?"

"Yeah. In fact, just two days ago, my second cousin was working at her part-time job at McCreepers. It was her first time at the counter, and there was a Zombie in line yelling at her. Zombies are super scary when they're hungry, and this Zombie was really hungry for his McBooger."

"So what happened," Steve asked.

"Well, he got his McBooger all right. . .with a side order of Creeper sauce. . .and Creeper entrails. . .and Creeper toes…"

"Uh. . .okay," Steve said while doing the eyebrow thing again.

"Well, dude, a crush is when you really like somebody, and when you find out she doesn't like you back, it feels like somebody took a pickaxe and smashed your heart into a million pieces. . . and it crushes your soul, for the like the rest of eternity."

"Seriously?"

"Uh. . .yeah!"

"Oh man, I think I'm in trouble," I said, thinking about Tibia.

"Well, you know what will help you not worry? An adventure!" cheered Steve.

"Huh?"

"I remember you were saying that you were going camping near the Forest Biome Cavern, right? Well, there's a swamp by there with a Witch that I want to visit. I need to get a special potion from her. Wanna come?"

"Yeah! Sounds awesome," I said.

To be honest, I was kinda scared.

Witches always creep me out.

But I needed to find something to get my mind off this crush.

Oh, man. . .I'm so doomed.

Sunday

Man, I'm really tired.

Setting up a tent is really hard work.

Especially when your whole family has no arms. . .

Seymour was too little to help out, and Ima just spent all her time tapping on her phone.

So, I had to do most of the work myself.

When I finished, I was really proud of my work, though.

But there sure was a lot of gunpowder left over. . .

19

I probably should've gone to the bathroom first.

Anyway, there's a tradition that we do as a family every year when we are at the caravan park. As a family, we bake some cookies and then go out and meet the neighbors.

Sometimes we get to meet some pretty cool mobs.

Like last year, we met a really cool Endermen family.

I got along really well with their kids, the Ender twins, Edgar and Ellen.

But, at night they would secretly teleport into different tents and move people's stuff.

Yeah, they didn't think that through very well.

There were a lot of Creeper families that year.

Or at least there were.

So wrong.

Anyway, we were at one of the last of our neighbors' tents.

We met a lot of mob families already, but none of them were super cool.

Oh, well, seems like it was going to be another boring year of camping. . .

KNOCK KNOCK.

"Jasper? Is that you?!!!"

"Harry?!!!"

"WHOAAAAAA!!!"

Monday

This summer vacation is going to be awesome!

That's because I just found out that my friend Harry O'Brien is my next-door neighbor.

Turns out that our parents thought that since we had been working hard at school all year, they wanted to surprise us.

Yeah, where they got that idea, I don't know.

But anyway, now I get to hang out with my best friend for the whole summer.

Sweet!

Now, being the master of the campsite, I showed Harry the dirtiest bathrooms, the coolest places to find squid in the lake and the best broken swings to use in the playground.

After the tour was done, we sat down to eat our lunch.

"URGH! Jalapeño sandwiches again?" groaned Harry as he unwrapped his lunch. "I am so tired of these."

"You wanna trade?"

"Sure."

Pffft.

I was happily munching away when I noticed Harry, normally a chatter box, was giving me a confused look.

"Dude, what's up? You smell different," Harry said, glaring at me.

I blinked. "What do you mean?"

"Dude, are you sick?" prodded Harry. "Smells like a mutant bog creature ate some rancid old cheese. . .made of toe jam."

HSSSSSSSSSSSS.

"Don't you start hissing at me! Come on, man. What's going on!"

"All right, all right! I, uh. . .been having a bad case of bubble guts," I finally said.

"Man, I knew something smelled off."

Wait. . .Harry doesn't even have a nose. . .so how does he. . .?

"Dude, isn't bubble guts like...dangerous for a Creeper?" Harry said.

"I don't know, I've never felt like this before."

"So did you figure out what's causing it?" Harry asked.

"Yeah...I think I have a crush on a girl."

Harry's eyes got even wider. His jaw almost dropped to the ground...and then...

"HAHAHAHAHAHAHA!!!"

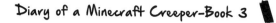

"Yeah, I know."

"HAHAHAHAHAHAHA!!!"

"Stop it. You know when I get embarrassed it makes me nervous."

"HAHAHAHAHAHAHA!!!"

PRRRRFFFFFTTTT!

"Ewwwwwww! Cough. . .cough, cough!"

"Your reaction was sure different than Steve's," I said.

"Who's Steve?" asked Harry, trying to catch his breath.

"Oh, Steve! You should definitely meet him. You guys kinda remind me of each other, but without the eyeballs," I said.

"Uh. . .okay. So when do I get to meet this guy?" Harry asked, finally stopping his guffaws.

"Why not tonight?"

Later that night, we were crowded around for dinner in the campsite. Mom made our favorite camp food, pumpkin stew!

"Oh, remember, kids, we're helping out at the annual Creeper fireworks this year," said Dad.

28

"Awww man! Do we have to?" Ima and I groaned.

"Yes, you do," Mom said. "You know its our family tradition which we do every year."

Now, don't get me wrong. The fireworks event is great. But I really, REALLY don't like preparing for it.

We have this tradition, that on the last Saturday of the camping trip, all the Creepers around the park prepare an amazing fireworks show. And each family is in charge of bringing a different color gunpowder. There's even a contest of who can make the brightest fireworks.

Well, I think I told you how Creepers make gunpowder.

But if you forgot, just know that it has something to do with our genetic makeup.

29

. . . And our poop.

Well, last year was the worst. We had to make green gunpowder.

We had to eat broccoli and brussel sprouts for a whole week.

So nasty.

We didn't win, either. A Creeper family a few tents down won.

They had the coolest rainbow fireworks you've ever seen.

They must've been eating Skittles for like a whole year, that's how bright their fireworks were.

I wonder what color we'll be doing this year?

Anyway, I glanced at the clock and it was almost time to meet Harry. So I tried to shove all my dinner in my mouth as possible.

"Slow down, Jasper! Why are you in such a rush?" asked Mom.

"Maybe he's worried the Ender Zombie might come snatch his dinner away," Dad sniggered.

"Wait…what?"

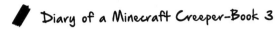

"Nah, Dad. He's probably just excited to be by himself so he could think about his crush," teased Ima.

HSSSSSS.

Monday Night

Harry got to the meeting spot with so much food in his mouth, I could barely see his glowing eyes.

We met by a huge tree near the playground.

You know, I never noticed how creepy playgrounds at the night are.

Then the wind started blowing and the swings start moving. . .

Prrrft.

Luckily, Harry came by and we began our adventure to find Steve.

When we got to where he was, we saw Steve punching a tree outside of his house.

"What's that weird dude doing?" Harry asked.

All of a sudden, when Steve saw us, his eyes popped out of his head.

It was weird. . .I thought only Zombies did that.

Steve was staring really hard at Harry.

And Harry was staring really hard at Steve.

Harry tried to break the ice, so he stuck his fist out for a fist pound.

Just as he did, Steve put out his hand for handshake.

No! Nooo! NOOOOOOOO!

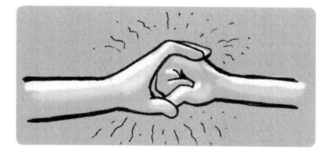

THE WORST, MOST CATACLYSMIC, EPIC FAIL EVER!

So for the next 20 minutes, they both tried switching from handshake to fist pump trying to get it right.

I felt so much cringe that my butt cheeks felt like they were going to explode.

I mean, I clenched so hard, I think I could've crushed a diamond in my back pocket.

"Hey, Steve! Why don't you tell Harry about why you're here?" I shouted, trying to reduce the effect of this epic cringe level event.

"Oh, I'm on a mission to find the Swamp Witch and get a special potion," Steve explained to Harry.

"What kind of potion?"

"You know, a healing potion."

"Huh? what so special about that," wondered Harry.

"Well, I have this really bright colored rash on my…"

"Whoa! Bro. . .T.M.I., dude, T.M.I.!"

Harry turned his head and gave me a look.

Oops.

But you know, in spite of the epic awkwardness, Harry and Steve got along really well.

They even started to finish each other's. . .sandwiches.

So weird.

Tuesday

Just after breakfast, Harry and I were walking around the beach near the campsite.

GRRRRRRRRR!

I tried to keep quiet, but I couldn't get control of my bodily functions.

"So who do you have a crush on?" sniggered Harry.

HSSSSSSS.

"Dude calm down. It's not something you can just avoid. Maybe talking about it will help."

HSSSSSSSSS.

"So tell me who it is?" teased Harry.

Breathe. . .Jasper. . .Breathe. . .You can do this. . .

Prrrffft.

"It's Tibia McRib. She's a new girl in my homeroom class and. . ."

"You like Tibia!"

Harry said it so loud that everybody could hear him for miles.

Then my stomach started up again.

GGGRRRRRRRRRRR.

Oh, man, this is bad. It's been five days since I felt this way. . .and the feeling is getting worse.

"Dude, why don't you stand on your head?" Harry said. "I heard that's supposed to help."

So then I stood upside-down for a little while.

It made me feel a little better. . .but it was sure hard to go to the bathroom.

When my Mom caught me standing upside-down she told me to stop.

She said something about getting too much gunpowder in my brain.

Anyway, Harry started making fun of my crush on Tibia.

HSSSSS.

But then, as we were walking by the beach we saw a huge Creeper.

"DUDE! IT'S BURT!" shouted Harry.

Then we ran up to him.

"Dude, what are you doing here?" I asked him.

"My parents couldn't book our normal vacation at Let It Rip Resort, so they decided to have the summer vacation here instead," shrugged Burt.

"Well, it's great to see you, man. Where you staying?" asked Harry.

"Over that way," nodded Burt toward the playground.

Harry and I followed the direction of his nod, and as we turned our heads, we couldn't believe what we saw.

"Hey, Jasper. Isn't that. . .?"

HSSSSSSSSS.

Yup. It was.

Tibia McRib in the flesh.

"Who's that good-looking Wither Skeleton boy she's with?" Harry asked.

HSSSSSSSSS.

"And why is she hugging him so tight?" Harry continued.

HSSSSSSSSS.

"Uh. . .I think I'm gonna be sick. . ."

Prrrffft.

Then everything went black.

Wednesday

I woke up today, and I couldn't stop thinking about Tibia.

Then my stomach started making noise again.

GRRRRRRRRRR!

I just kept thinking, *why was she hugging that Wither Skeleton kid? How did they meet? And are they like. . .DATING?*

Oh, man, I think I'm going to explode.

PLOP!

Well, I didn't explode.

So after I cleaned myself up, I went to see Harry.

"Dude, what am I going to do? Tibia has the hots for a Wither skeleton," I said. "Not to mention, that he's really tall, dark and bony. How am I going to compete with that?"

"Yeah, that guys really big-boned too," Harry said.

"Yeah, thanks."

HSSSSSS.

Then Steve walked up to where we were and gave me and Harry a high-five.

But I didn't have the energy to high five Steve, though. . .

. . .Or the arms.

"What's crackin', guys?" Steve said.

"My, heart! That's what! Sniff. . .sniff."

45

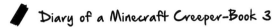
"What's the matter with Jasper?" Steve asked Harry.

"He just saw the love of his life hanging with another dude."

"Whoa, that's cold, bro."

HSSSSSS.

"Like I told you. . .they don't call it a crush for nothing."

Prffft.

"Hey, I got a great idea!" Steve said. "Why don't you ask the Witch for a love potion? I'm sure the Witch has one of those hanging around."

"That's a great idea, man," Harry said. "That'll make Tibia fall in love with you, and Wither boy won't stand a chance."

"Sniff. . .sniff. . .Really? You think she would have a potion for me?"

"Yeah, man. No sweat," Steve said. "Witches are always making love potions. It's the only way they can get husbands because they're so. . .you know. . .mugly."

You know, I always wondered how the witch in my neighborhood got married. It's like one day she was all 'CACKLE – CACKLE – CACKLE!' and the next minute she brought this guy home.

"Whoa!"

Love potion, huh. . .I get it.

"All right, guys, I'm in!"

Thursday

I told Burt about our plan, and he was all in.

The plan was for Harry, Burt, and me to sneak out of the campsite after dinner and go see the Witch.

But before we left, Mom made a lot of pumpkin pie, so I had to stay for that.

Yeah, I think my family is in charge of the orange fireworks this year.

YES!

Anyway, Burt was already at the tree when I got there.

Then Harry and I warned Burt about Steve.

49

We weren't sure how he'd react if he saw a human coming out of the cave.

The good thing is that Steve knew exactly how to deal with Creepers. He's cool like that.

"Hey, Jasper's Creeper friend. I'm Steve, and I come in peace."

Then Steve put his hand under his armpit and. . .

PRRFFT! PRRFFT! PRRFFT!

We all looked at Burt. We weren't sure what he was gonna do.

Then he burst out laughing. And the rest was history.

"Yo! Let's get going," shouted Harry as he walked toward us with his eyes lit up.

It's a good thing, too. I totally forgot my flashlight.

So we finally made it into the Forest.

Once we met Steve, he grabbed his pack on got ready for our adventure of a lifetime.

He took out his map and started leading the way.

So Steve and Harry led the way, while me and Burt hopped at the back.

Yeah, Creepers generally aren't the bravest apples in the bunch.

And it didn't help walking in the dark and hearing the howling wind and rustling leaves.

Prrffft.

"Hold up guys!" shouted Steve.

Then Steve walked behind me and Burt and started dusting the floor for gunpowder.

"Hey, we might need some TNT on our adventure," Steve said.

So wrong.

"Hey, I think I found the Witch's hut!" Harry shouted.

Without a word, Steve started running through the trees with Harry right behind him.

Burt and me tried to keep up, but Creepers don't run very well.

I think it has something to do with our tiny little legs. . . and being so top-heavy.

By the time Burt and I hopped our way out of the trees, Steve and Harry were already at the hut door.

Oh, man.

HSSSSSSS.

Harry turned around. "Hey, calm down, guys. Just breathe. . .Breathe. . ."

HSSSSSSS.

All of a sudden. . .

"HAHAHAHAHAHA!"

"WHAT THE WHAT'N WHAT, WAS THAT?"
Burt blurted.

Burt and I looked up slowly.

And there in front of us was what looked like a humongous nose with a face on it. . .

Oh. . .and it had a huge unibrow.

"It's the Witch!" Harry blurted.

Whoa. I've never seen a Witch up close before.

And the guys weren't kidding. She was butt-ugly.

As she came closer to us, I saw that her hair was green.

55

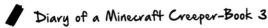

And it was moving. . .Blech!

Then she started staring me down with her beady eyes, and my stomach started rumbling again.

"HAHAHAHAHAHA!" she cackled.

SHSSSSSSSSSSSSS.

BOOOOOOOM!!!!

Then everything went black.

Thursday, Later That Night

I woke up to Steve and Harry hovering over me.

I got up and looked around and saw a bubbling cauldron.

"Oh man. . .what happened?" I asked the guys.

"Uh. . .you exploded," said Steve.

"What?!!!"

"Yeah, man, you like blew Creeper chunks all over the room," Steve said.

"Seriously?!!!"

"Yeah, dude, I got some in my mouth too," Harry said as he hocked a loogie and spit it across the room.

"How come I'm still in one piece?"

"Matilda the Witch cast a spell and put you back together," smiled Steve.

Then the Witch looked at me and gave me a toothless smile.

Blech!

"Hey, where's Burt? Did he. . ." I asked.

"Naw, he's okay. He's over there," Harry said, pointing to the bathroom. "Yeah, he blew chunks the other way."

Ewwww!

"Oh, I am so sorry I frightened you, sweet pea," apologized Matilda.

She is so weird.

"Uh. . .no problem. . .Ms. Matilda," I said.

"Well, I think you are very brave for coming with your friends to find me. Steve has already told me about his rash, but he said you wanted to ask me something too."

"Uh. . .yeah. . .um. . .you wouldn't happen to have a potion that can make a girl fall in love with you, do you?"

"Ah, the LOVE potion!" exclaimed Matilda.

"HAHAHAHAHAHA!"

Man, I really wish she wouldn't do that.

HSSSSSSSSSSSS.

"Ah, what you want is called the Legendary Offer of Valiant Effort potion," Matilda said. "Or you can just call it. . .The Love Brew."

"Whoa!" we all said.

"Yes. . .it is the most powerful potion in all of Minecraft. And it is capable of ensnaring nearly any mob in an immobilizing love."

"Whoa!"

"Unfortunately, I don't have the main ingredient to make it," she said.

"Awwwwww!"

"Well, what is it that you need? Maybe we can get it," Steve said.

"Well, the main ingredient is the eye of a special Spider that you can only find in the Carnivorous Caves," she continued.

Gulp!

"What makes this Spider so special?" Steve asked.

"Well, this Spider is as old as Minecraft itself. It was one of the first mobs to ever be created by the Gods of Mojang."

"Seriously?"

"Yes, they really didn't know what they were doing back then. That is why it is known as... The Barking Spider!"

"HAHAHAHAHAHA!"

Prrrffft.

"So, I'm sorry, kids. No eye, no love potion," the Witch said. "But I do have a friendship potion if you don't mind landing in the friend zone."

"Noooooooo!" we all gasped.

"Perfect, now I'll never have Tibia McRib as my girlfriend," I said.

"Aw, don't worry, Jay, I'll go to the Carnivorous Caves and help you get the Spider eye," Steve said.

"You can count me in, too," Harry said.

"Ssssame here," Burt said with a lisp.

Wow, I've got like the coolest friends in the whole world.

Alright Barking Spider, here we come!

Friday

After dinner, Burt, Harry and me met up to head to Steve's lair. It was time to come up with a game plan.

"From what I know of caves, the best way to make it through a cave is to know where you're going," said Steve.

Burt and I were quiet.

Yeah, Creepers don't like caves.

As we were getting ready, I decided to make sure to make a quick deposit before going on our adventure.

Yeah, I didn't want my stomach acting up again and ruining things.

So, as I was coming out of the bathroom, I heard a rustle behind me.

HSSSSSSSSS.

"Oh, you must be Jasper. I've heard a lot about you," came a voice form behind the bush.

What, another talking bush?

Then I turned around and saw a Wither Skeleton pop out of the bush.

"Hi, I'm Tobias Boneyparts. . .but you can call me Toby."

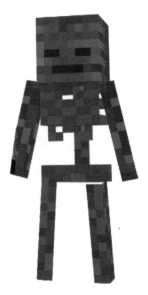

Oh, Man! It's the Wither kid I saw hugging Tibia!

"Uh. . .Hey. . .Toby. . .uh. . .what are you doing around here?"

"Just looking for the bathroom," he said as he rubbed his bony stomach.

"That camp food really gave me the runs. So I need to talk to a man about a mule, if you know what I mean."

"He. . .he. . .he. . ." I laughed nervously.

"Yeah, I just finished dropping off the kids at the pool," I said.

"What?"

"Nothing. So. . .uh, where's Tibia?" I asked Tobias as my voice started cracking.

"She's inside. Did you want me to call her?"

"Uh, no! No, no, no, no, no, no!"

Then we stood there in awkward silence for a while.

I would've twiddled my thumbs. If I had any.

"Um. . .okay, so if you wouldn't mind, I need to go visit Uncle Grumpy," Tobias said.

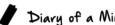

"Oh, yeah, man. Build yourself a log cabin while you're at it."

"What?"

"Nothing...nothing."

Then as Tobias walked in the bathroom, I could hear more rustling behind me.

When I turned around, I couldn't believe my eyes.

"Hi, Jasper."

OH, MY GOSH! WHAT THE WHAT?

"Oh. . .hi, Tibia! Uh. . .what brings you out tonight? He. . .he. . ."

GRRRRRRRRRR!

Shhh! I said to my stomach, hoping Tibia didn't hear that.

"Uh, Jasper, is everything okay?" Tibia asked as she threw her long flowing hair back in the swaying wind.

"Uh. . .it's fine. . .um, I just needed to drop some friends off at the pool. . .he. . .he."

"What?"

GRRRRRRRRRR!

"Uh, you know, just taking the Browns to the Super Bowl. He. He."

GRRRRRRRRRR!

"Huh?"

"You know, just negotiating the release of some chocolate hostages. He. He. He."

GRRRRRRRRRR!

Tibia just looked at me with that confused look Steve usually gives me.

"Are you sure you're alright?"

"Yeah. . .yeah. . .I'll see you later, bye," I said, running out of there as fast as I could.

So much for love. . .

Sigh.

Saturday

Early this morning, we started packing and getting ready for the cave.

Harry and Steve carried most of the gear since Burt and I didn't have . . .arms.

Anyway, luckily Steve was ready for this mission because he packed everything:

* Rope

* Empty bottle

* Pickaxe

* Iron sword

Then Steve brought out the map of the cave.

"Oh, man, that cave is massive!" Harry said. "How are we going to cover all that ground?"

"I think the best way is to split up," explained Steve. "Burt and Harry, you guys go that way. Me and Jasper will go this way," Steve said.

"Sounds like a plan," we all said.

"Let's do this."

Steve and I got to the mouth of the cave, and I could swear I heard a noise inside.

"Uh. . .are there any cats in there?" I asked Steve.

"Don't worry, dude," Steve said. "If there are any cats, they'll probably be friendly," he said, pulling out his sword for some reason.

HSSSSSSS.

Saturday Afternoon

Steve and I had been walking around the cave for maybe an hour.

No Spider. Zilch.

So much for my Love Brew.

"What are we going to do if we can't find the Spider?" I asked Steve.

"There's a reason they call it a crush, you know," replied Steve.

Not what I wanted to hear.

All of a sudden. . .

ARRRRRRRROOOOOOOO!

HSSSSSSSS.

"Dude, what was that?" I whispered to Steve.

"I dunno, but I think we should check it out," said Steve the Brave.

ARRRFFFFFF! ARRRFFFFFF!
ARRRRRRRRROOOOOOOOOOOO!

HSSSSSSSSSSSSSSSSSS.

And at that moment, I started to realize that maybe I'm too young to have a girlfriend. Or maybe having a girlfriend is not what it's cracked up to be. . .or maybe having a girlfriend is probably full of all kinds of drama. . .

Yeah, all kinds of things flash in your mind when you're about to die.

ARRRFFFFFF! ARRRFFFFFF! ARRRRRRRRROOOOOOOOOOOO!

I didn't want to admit it, but I knew we found what we were looking for.

So, as we got closer, the barking and howling got louder and louder.

PRRRRFFFFFTTTT.

HSSSSSSSS.

"Jasper, please, not now," pleaded Steve while trying to hold his breath.

But it wasn't me. And there was only one other Creeper in the cave.

And right when we reached the lava pit, we found Burt and Harry being attacked by a giant Mutant Spider!

"WHAT THE WHAT?!!!!" I yelled.

Suddenly, Steve started waving his arms and yelling at the top of his voice.

"ARROOOOOOOOO!" howled Steve, trying to get the Spider's attention.

Then the Giant Mutant Spider turned around and started running toward Steve and me.

"AAAAAAHHH!!!!"

I hopped over to where Burt and Harry were to keep from getting eaten by the Spider.

"Burt! Are you okay?" I asked him. Then I saw my buddy Harry on the floor.

"Harry!"

Harry was unconscious. . .which was a bummer because we could've really used his heat vision right now.

Harry is funny about his heat vision. I think it's because he can't control it.

It normally only comes out when he's really mad or when he's constipated.

Yeah, we learned the hard way not to get him mad when he's constipated.

Talk about dirty dynamite. . .

Anyway, Burt was hissing really loud. . .I think he was at his breaking point!

I helped Burt up and tried to wake Harry, while Steve was distracting the Giant Mutant Spider.

KRESH!

Steve threw a potion of Confusion at the Spider, which distracted him for a minute.

Then he ran over to us to help us with Harry.

"Hey, Jasper, what's a Creeper's favorite subject at school?" Steve said quickly.

"Huh?"

He didn't even wait for me to reply before blurting out, "Hissssss-tory."

"Tee hee," I laughed.

Prrrft.

Suddenly, Harry jumped up off the ground.

"EEEWWWWW, what was that?" Harry asked as he was holding his face where I think his nose would be.

"It smells like a butt wrapped in bacon served in a bowl of moldy cottage cheese!" Harry said.

"Sorry, bro, we needed you in this battle," Steve said.

So embarrassing.

Then Steve gave Harry a nod, and they quickly spun around to go back and battle the Spider.

Man, my friends are so cool. They're like. . .action heroes!

Tzzzzzzzzzzzzzzzzt.

Harry started using his heat vision to try and corner the spider.

I guess my toot must've activated it.

Then, I saw Steve grab his Sword and charge toward the Spider.

FWWWWOOOOON.

ARRRRRRROOOOOOOO!

Suddenly, out popped one of the Spiders eyes!

And then Harry jumped up and caught it right before it fell into the lava pit.

82

As the Spider retreated to patch itself up, the guys raced back to where we were.

"All right, guys, time to get outta here," Steve said.

Then Steve swung his backpack forward and rummaged through it.

He then threw some TNT in front of us.

"All right, step two in the plan!" yelled Steve.

Burt and I nodded at each other. We jumped on the rock platform that Harry was putting the TNT under.

"Here, Jasper, you hold the Spider eye," Harry said as he was finishing placing the TNT.

Once we were all on the platform, Harry focused his heat vision on the TNT.

Then the Spider started running toward us with its fangs out and screaming at the top of its lungs.

83

ARRRFFFFFF! ARRRFFFFFF! ARRRRRRRRROOOOOOOOOOOO!

"Hurry, Harry!" we yelled.

"EVERYBODY HOLD ON!" shouted Steve.

TZZZZZZZTTTTT.

BOOOOOOOOM!

The platform skyrocketed us up through the giant hole at the top of the cave, that went all the way to the surface.

ARRRRRRRRROOOOOOOOOOOO!

We could hear the Spider in the background as its howls grew fainter and fainter.

"Yeah! We did it!" We all started yelling and high-fiving each other.

I was so happy I wanted to join in.

So, I jumped on my head and high-fived the guys all around, like a boss.

Yeah!

I was so happy, I even started doing flips on the platform too.

Then suddenly. . .

Everything started going in slow motion. . .

"JJJJJAAAASSSSSPPPPERRRRR! WATCH OUT!"

Then I slowly saw the spider's eye tumble out of my pocket and down the mouth of the cave.

"NOOOOOOOOO!"

We all jumped to the edge of the platform to try to catch it, but we were too late.

Then we saw the spider's eye fall down into the cave, then into the lava pit and sink.

TSSSSSSSS.

Saturday Night

We finally made it to the surface, all in one piece.

But I was really sad.

My one chance to find love in the bony arms of the girl of my dreams was totally crushed.

Oh . . .now I get it.

. . .CRUSHED.

"Waaaaaaaahhhh!"

All the guys patted me on the back and tried to encourage me.

"Hey, at least we made it back alive," Harry said.

"Yeah, at least we have a story to tell at school," Burt said.

"Yeah, at least we had an adventure we'll never forget," Steve said.

Yeah, the guys were right.

But, man, I still felt lousy.

The good news was that we made it back just in time for the annual Creeper firework spectacular.

We all hopped toward the beach where all our families and the other mobs were waiting with their fireworks.

Blazes were all around to help light up the gunpowder. And as they started, the night sky started to light up, one firework at a time.

It was awesome.

Except. . .I was still really sad.

It would've been really nice to be with my new girlfriend watching the fireworks, I thought.

Sniff. . .sniff.

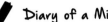

"Hey, Jasper, are you all right," whispered a voice behind me.

All of a sudden, when I turned around, I couldn't believe my eyes.

It was Tibia McRib, in the flesh. . .or I mean in the. . .uh. . .you know what I mean.

"Uh. . .I'm okay," I said, trying to wipe the tears from my face. . .which was kind of impossible.

"You sure are sensitive," Tibia said.

And then she smiled at me.

All of a sudden, I started to get that weird feeling in my stomach again. . .except this time, it felt more like butterflies. . .

But, then suddenly, Tobias came by.

"Hey, Tibia."

"Oh, hi, Tobias."

Urgh! so much for my romantic moment, I thought.

"Oh, hey, Jasper, have you met my cousin, Tobias?" Tibia said.

"Yeah, we met at the. . .Wait. . .What?!!!"

"Tobias, this is my friend Jasper. He's one of the coolest kids in school," she said, giving me a weird look with her big, beautiful eye sockets.

"Yeah, we met by the bathroom," Toby said. "Hey, how are those kids you dropped off at the pool doing?"

"Uh. . .their great. Cough. Cough."

"Hey, Jasper. I wanted to ask you if you wanted to watch the fireworks with me," Tibia asked me.

91

"Uh. . .sure," I said, trying not to explode.

Then she grabbed my hand, and we walked over to where some of the other couples were sitting.

GRRRRRRRRRR!

"What's that?" Tibia asked.

"Nothing. . .just nothing."

Sunday

So, we're all heading back home today.

And I've got to say, this has been the best summer vacation of my life.

It couldn't have been any better.

I mean, I got a chance to hang with my best buds for the whole summer.

And, I got a chance to meet a real-life Witch.

And, I got a chance to go on an epic adventure, and I survived to tell the tale.

And, I got a chance to watch an amazing fireworks show. . .which we won by the way.

Yeah, orange is the new rainbow around here.

93

And best of all, I got a chance to go on a date with the most amazing girl in all of Minecraft.

It was awesome!

I really hope Tibia will go out with me again, though.

I wasn't sure if she got weirded out by all the noises I was making.

I just told her I had a barking spider in my pocket, which she weirdly said she totally understood.

But she did say that she would come to my birthday party next week, so I think we're cool.

Oh yeah, it's my birthday next week.

And I turn twelve years old.

Hmm. I've never been twelve before. I wonder what that's gonna be like.

Well, I guess we'll have to wait till my birthday to find out. . .

HSSSSS.

THE END

Find out What
Happens Next in...

Diary of a Minecraft Creeper Book 4
"Breaking Wind"

Get Your Copy on Amazon Today!

If you really liked this book, please tell a friend. I'm sure they will be happy you told them about it.

Leave Us a Review Too

Please support us by leaving a review. The more reviews we get the more books we will write!

Check Out Our Other Books from Pixel Kid Publishing

The Diary of a Minecraft Creeper
Book Series

Get The Entire Series on
Amazon Today!

The Diary of a Minecraft Enderman
Book Series

Get The Entire Series on Amazon Today!

Made in the USA
Lexington, KY
29 October 2018